HANDBOOKS OF EUROPEAN NATIONAL DANCES

EDITED BY
VIOLET ALFORD

DANCES OF FINLAND

Plate 1
South Bothnia

DANCES of FINLAND

YNGVAR HEIKEL

AND

ANNI COLLAN

NOVERRE PRESS

ILLUSTRATED BY
VALERIE PRENTIS
MUSIC ARRANGED FOR THE PIANO BY
FERDINAND RAUTER

First published in 1948
This edition published in 2021 by
The Noverre Press
Southwold House
Isington Road
Binsted
GU34 4PH

ISBN 978-1-906830-97-7

CONTENTS

Illustrations in Colour, pages 2, 19, 30, 31
Map of Finland, page 6

T<small>HIS</small> great country of lakes and forests is called in its own tongue Suomi. Long years of foreign rule gave the country its other name, and as Finland it is generally known still. Suomi, with its ancient tongue, which does not belong to the Indo-European family of languages, nevertheless shares in the widespread Indo-European folk culture, as we shall see. The first reference to Finnish dancing occurs very early in most interesting verse.

The Finnish national epic, Kalevala, tells how Kyllikki, carried off by the young hero Lemminkäinen while dancing with the maidens, makes a condition before her marriage: he must never wage war any more. Lemminkäinen promises but makes a condition himself, recited in the lovely Kalevala metre, which is runic, eight-syllable verse, familiar to Anglo-Saxon ears in Longfellow's *Hiawatha:*

> *But thyself on oath must pledge thee,*
> *Not to wander to the village,*
> *Whether for the love of dancing,*
> *Or to loiter in the pathways.*

This reference to dancing comes to us probably from the twelfth century or earlier, when the Chain dance was already circling. In early days only the girls 'carolled', singing the ballads or epics, as in all Northern and Western countries of Europe. A faint reflection of this still lingers in Finland as in many another countryside, in the notion that, once married, a girl must dance no more. Later both girls and men took part in the Chain, sung words became lyrical and erotic. Later again, the person in the middle of the Ring or closed Chain selects a partner, with whom he or she swings round for a time. The antique Chain begins to break into the Pair dance. These Chains have been preserved in some regions, have met and overlapped the influx of dances from foreign parts.

Again, as in many another country, the Finnish folk dances of today were the ballroom dances of yesterday. They came to Finnish aristocratic and rich middle-class houses carried on the waves of fashion. Their names denote their origins—Anglaise, Française, Quadrilles called French, Swedish and Russian, and latterly even a Pas d'Espagne, a Pair dance to a 3/4 air of possible Spanish origin bringing with it a faint breath of the South. The fashionable Minuet came in its great days, and left at least its name behind it. All these went out of fashion, but, changing by degrees to the taste of the peasants, keep their once-fashionable names and are still danced by them today.

Other dances seem to have been created by the country folk themselves, inspired by what they saw around them. Those on the sea coast evolved the Seals' Jump, fishermen made a Net-dragging dance, those who lived in the forests turned to forest creatures and gave us a Bear's dance, Hare-hunting, The Grey Bird, The Sparrow's Song. Village people saw choreographical possibilities in everyday life, so we have Making Coffee, The Cat's Whiskers, The Spool; while farmworkers like miming their own work and give us The Carter, The Reaping Dance, Potato-Tops, The Cowman.

The Anglaise forms are supposed to have come from England, and indeed suggest an enlargement of English country dance figures, having two couples a side instead of one in a Square. The original Anglaise, whatever it may have been, was known to country people by 1790 or there-abouts. There is also an example of the solo Stick dance, Tikkuristi, after the style of the English Bacca Pipes Jig and the many similar European forms, over two sticks crossed on the ground. Another name for Tikkuristi is Slinkepass, an amusing folk corruption of *Cinquepace*, Cinq pas. Other dances bear local names, others are danced to satirical verses and are called after them. One such is Taneli, one-eyed Taneli, who has to endure the contempt of four girls, administered in the ruthless manner of the folk, who are all too ready to despise physical disabilities. Another is Riitta, mocked for her club-foot, and again the girl from Forssa, whose morals are shown up with piercing clarity in the satirical verse that accompanies it. Miming grows easily round such rhymes.

⚜ POLKA AND POLSKA ⚜

Suomi seems to have welcomed this Central European dance with open arms—if indeed the two names denote the same dance. The Polka burst into ballrooms about 1840 or a little earlier, and has always been claimed by Poland as one of her traditional dances which travelled abroad, though Czechoslovakia makes her claim heard too as the original home of a dance called Pùlka. It came into the ballroom as a Pair dance, became a country Pair dance, and is cherished now in several lands as an original folk dance of their own, as in Denmark, Switzerland and the Netherlands, for instance.

The word Polska in Polish means Poland, and in Finland a variety of forms are called by this name. They are generally in 3/4, though not Waltz rhythm, as opposed to the 2/4 of the Polka, and are sometimes a Pair dance, but just as often a Figure dance by four couples or more standing in Square or Round formation. One, the Hollolan Polska, or The Nine Persons, is in three lines of three, one line facing down, the other two facing up, one behind the other. Polska therefore has no certain meaning in Finland. It was used as an introduction to the banquet until the Waltz came in and pushed it into a secondary position, when it

9

became the last dance, and was called the Parting Polska. Then when young people disdained knowledge of it it became the Old Men's Polska, like the somewhat derogatory Danse des Vieux of so many French villages.

❧ THE PURPURI ❧

The 'biggest' of Finland's dances is the Purpuri, and a real potpourri it is, comprising all sorts of figures—up to nine in Nyland, diminishing in number in the Eastern villages until finally there is but one. The figures are generally named Vals, Russian Quadrille, Polska, March, though they hardly conform to the dances they are named after— a constant snare to the dance-collector in every country of Europe. Sometimes eight couples take part beginning in Square formation. The tempo changes with every figure, each one of which has its own tune, and steps comprise stamping, springing, promenading, according to the figure. Altogether an intricate and prolonged composite dance.

❧ THE EASTERN REGION ❧

Karelia, the south-eastern province of Suomi, on the Gulf of Finland, shows characteristics of its own, somewhat reflecting the dances of its great dancing neighbour. In these villages we find The Cossack, Kaseska, and The Squatting Russian. Here also is the Contra or Cross-Contra, a Square for eight couples, who constantly cross and recross in various patterns. The final figure is Ripatska, in which a man performs the Cossack squatting step. When called the Cross Dance it takes on a curious religious touch, and a verse is sometimes sung to its movements:

> Christ is riding to the Church on a grey horse.
> Let us dance the Cross Dance, the King of all dances.

Perhaps of old it was used as a religious Processional.

Those who have not lived through a northern winter can hardly understand the relief, the uplifting of the spirit when the sun rises again above the horizon. Since Christianity was brought to them, the spring festivals of the Finns have been Whitsuntide and Ascension Day in the south-west of Suomi.

In the east of the country celebrations centre round the ancient Midsummer, the Summer Solstice festival of pre-Christian times, now hailed as St. John the Baptist's Day. On the eves of these festivals bonfires burn in every village, believed today, as of old, to drive away evil spirits and sickness. In some places a Midsummer pole, often of a great height, is erected, beautifully decorated with garlands of greenery and with flowers. Round the fires and round the poles the people dance Rounds and Pair dances until the morning.

⚜ *A FINNISH WEDDING* ⚜

We must put some of these dances into action, and look at the customs surrounding them, and at the people in their bright, striped dresses coming to enjoy them. Great preparations were made, and still are when possible, and a marriage was usually arranged for the long, light days when the North knows no night. The women of the house prepared all sorts of fatted creatures, the master of the house brought drinks from the nearest town, and there was always home-brewed beer, thick and sweet. The whole house was cleaned, and all the outbuildings, for every inch of space would be used. The house was next decorated, a triumphal arch raised; the bath-house, an essential to all Finnish dwellings, decked with greenery and flowers, while the old bath attendant prepared the bath for the bride and for all the company too.

The chief bridesmaid now begins to attire the bride, and other girls make her myrtle-wreath, and tie rosettes of white tulle to the wreaths for the bridegroom, the bridesmaids and groomsmen. Nowadays the conventional white, like the conventional Waltz, has crept into weddings, but of old the bride was crowned with the bridal crown standing high at the back of her head, all glittering with beads and gold and silver paper like the decorations on a Christmas tree. It rested on a little cap of beautiful white lace softening the cheeks; long ribbons hung from the crown down the back.

The musicians arrive, the bridegroom and his escorting men appear in two-wheeled wagons and are received with music. Guests come into view far off, and each time a vehicle appears on the road the musicians greet it with the Bridal March. The clergyman of the parish arrives and, if the weather is true midsummer weather, the ceremony takes place in the courtyard. A bright rug and footstools are placed in an arbour of young birch trees, and the bridal pair walks to it along a carpet strewn with flowers. Four men now raise a coloured shawl as a canopy over their heads, and as in the bridal crown we see here the widespread Indo-European marriage ceremony, best known to us through the tradition of ancient Rome. Here in the far North it is as true to type as on the slopes of the Pyrenees. A long, long feast follows the religious rite, the guests sitting strictly according to custom, the clergyman next the bridegroom, the chief bridesmaid next the bride and so on. The feast comprises succulent northern dishes, salmon, home-cured hams, and the Finnish barley porridge cooked in milk for four hours and eaten with cream. Grace is sung, speeches and drinking begin, the young guests rise to dance. Mazurka and Polka open the ball, elders join in Waltz and Purpuri. In Swedish-speaking districts the canopy-holders, the bridal pair and attendants dance Minuet and Polska before the guests join in; in some other districts we see the long Purpuri as the 'canopy dance'.

All the village comes to look on, and these uninvited guests now 'shout the bride out' several times. Their imperious summons must by no means be disobeyed. Out then she comes in all her finery, finer still if the ancient crown is sparkling on her head, to show herself to these people. They too must dance, and a special outhouse is reserved for them. At midnight the vicar says good-bye, the elders begin to disappear, but the dance goes on, and on and on. At last the bride is blindfolded, the girls dance round her rapidly, their hearts beating with anxiety, for whoever she catches in the circling ring will be the next bride. The bridegroom officiates in this half-believed divination for a ring of men. The crown is 'danced off' and the exhausted bridal pair creeps away at last.

Next day a kerchief is put on to show the young wife's new status. And now her dancing days are supposed to be done, but perhaps she manages a Polka now and then. Festivities go on all that day, until the pair leave for their new home—a sight worth seeing. Off they drive, the bridal couple first, the musicians next, playing their loudest through villages, saving their breath in the forest. All the friends follow, harness shining, horses groomed till they shine too. The bridegroom's parents, oddly enough, do not attend the ceremony, but stay at home preparing yet another feast. Sometimes the bride will pour a cup of water over her head 'for luck', but in reality as a fertilising, beneficent magic. Sometimes she throws money into the house before entering—another piece of sympathetic magic, that money may never lack. The young man lifts his wife from the cart or sleigh on to a carpet—doubtless he once used to lift her over the threshold into the new home. Now reverting to their Christian upbringing they kneel to recite the Lord's Prayer, and all sing a hymn. But later all unknowingly she falls back again, touches the oven—as the Southern bride touches the chain of the hanging pot, and the Roman bride paid honour to the family Penates. The feasting now begins all over again. Next evening the guests really do drive off, having danced a final Polka; 'Long as a wedding in Karelia' says a Finnish proverb most truly.

✳ THE SWEDISH-SPEAKING DISTRICTS ✳

These districts are on the seaboard, the coast of the Gulf of Bothnia and the Åland Islands containing the greatest number of Swedish-speaking people. The coastline looking across the Gulf of Finland contains patches of Swedish-speaking people also. Most of their dances are like the Finnish dances, were once ballroom dances and have become traditional amongst the people. Many of these have been altered out of recognition, yet retain some famous name such as Minuet. No longer a stately ballroom piece for one or two couples, it is now a Longways Country dance, men and women facing each other, and it had, we know, arrived at that formation by the early part of the nineteenth century. It is a favourite at local festivities, and a fine sight it is in some villages near Kristinestad, S.W. Bothnia, where the regional costumes are still worn. At weddings it is performed with solemnity, not a smile to be seen. But it should be followed by a lively Polska with stamping and shouting to let off high spirits. The Polska, often called Trinndans, Round Dance, has been mentioned in detail already, and in these Swedish-speaking districts displays the same characteristics as in Suomi, varying from a dance for two or three people to one for two or more couples, which ends in a ring.

A long and complicated dance up to eighteen figures is the Stora Själen, the Big Winding, found in Eastern Nyland. Various Engelska are widely spread and appear in several forms. When they take a Longways form, men and women facing each other as in Sex Man Engelska, Six Pairs, it is easy to believe they arrived in Finland as an English country dance, for we know this type travelled and became fashionable all over Western Europe. Some, the Kökar

Engelska for instance, have what well may be Scottish or Northern English tunes, but others move right away from English forms. The Fyrkanter, with promenades, setting to partners and chaine anglaise or hey, is probably of English country dance extraction. As in Suomi people are fond of miming the animals they are familiar with, and have invented such little dances as the Seals' Jump, the Crow Dance and the Fly Dance. These seem to have no ritual foundation, however, no traditional date or costume.

The Bear Dance, however, must come into the ritual category for it is performed on the second day of wedding festivities. Two men dress in fur, skin caps and gloves, and grasping a pole—for of course the dancing-bear idea has crept in—dance inside a space marked off by benches. The guests feed the bears with bread, sugar and brandy. Fights ensue if not enough drink is given. In many countries the bear is a symbol of fecundity, and here, at a marriage, appears to have that meaning.

Since 1906 a great work has been proceeding in the revival of Swedish folk culture in Finland by the Brage Society. It concerns itself not only with dance and music, but with poetry, traditional games, customs and costumes. Folk dance has been systematically taught where it was dying, the collecting and noting of dances and airs proceed, and results are published by the Brage Society.

MUSIC

We have seen that singing accompanied the primitive Chain dance of Suomi. An interesting old instrument played by ancient Finnish musicians, and in use right into the eighteenth century, is the *kantele*. Its original purpose was to accompany singers of tunes. It is a beautiful thing, of wood slightly decorated in chip ornament, a long triangle in shape, originally with five strings. The tuning keys occupy the shortest of the three sides. It is laid on a table like a zither, but the strings are plucked. Like the Celtic harp in Scotland this old instrument is enjoying a new lease of life, new models are being made, and modern musicians are using up to thirty strings. So from a folk product it has become a musical instrument of art and—following the regular shuttle movement between folk and non-folk—the people have discarded it for the violin.

Fiddle and clarinet have made a lively accompaniment for a century or more; today, as everywhere, the accordion has pushed its way into the band. Country musicians were self-taught men, famous for musical memory, even for virtuosity. Ensembles were not uncommon, violin, clarinet and the old kantele. Ten thousand dance tunes have been collected in the country, and amongst the best of these are the Polska airs.

COSTUME

Folk costume has a long history in Suomi, beginning with the dresses found in the funerary barrows, dating from about A.D. 1000 to 1200. But we must turn to the eighteenth century when Gustav III of Sweden reigned over both countries. He attempted to stem the luxury of fashion, and paternally created a dress suitable to the cold climate. He himself set an example and insisted on his Court doing likewise. Thus a new national dress came into use, which, as always, was subjected to changes according to fashion and region.

Two groups of costume can be descried, the Eastern in Karelia, the Western over the rest of the country. The Eastern group preserved tradition well, for women still wear a medieval white head-dress in South Karelia, the long white tunic in the Karelian Isthmus, even carry the sheathed knife in the belt for defence, and the needlecase and purse for domestic use. Women wear a veil, varying from village to village, unmarried girls a head-braid of red wool decorated with bright studs. Skirts are of plain woollen stuff with red borders, aprons are embroidered, and a wide short cloak keeps the wearer warm.

Men wrap themselves in white or light grey cloaks; of old their whole costume was of these colours, later darkening to blue and brown. Their stockings are red or white.

The Western group shows more colour: stripes, sometimes horizontal but generally vertical, brighten skirts and aprons, a sleeveless bodice goes over a white blouse, and a sleeved jacket completes the dress but often is not worn, so that white sleeves become a usual feature. Caps are of all sorts of shapes and colours, in some regions decorated with beautiful lace falling softly over the cheeks.

The Swedish-speaking districts too love stripes, scarlet and green, scarlet and black; skirt, apron and sleeveless bodice may all be striped. The stockings are coloured, and low black shoes, often buckled, go with them. A characteristic feature is an embroidered pocket hanging at the waist. One costume, that of Munsala, East Bothnia, is chiefly blue, a rare colour in folk costume.

Men's dress is now a fashion of the last century, with either knee-breeches or trousers, low buckled shoes, and a buckled belt round the waist. Shirts are white, often richly embroidered, leather caps with woollen stitching have taken the place of the old tall hat of ceremony.

All over the country a lively interest in traditional costume exists, and a general revival of it for summer festivals has had a good deal of success. Lovely traditional costumes for both sexes, long seen only in museums, are reappearing all over the countryside.

This is the merest résumé of a wide and detailed subject, and the costumes here illustrated should be studied with the greatest care. Any of these are correct for the dances given, for, as has been seen, there are very few purely local dances in this great land.

WHERE DANCING MAY BE SEEN

✳✳✳✳✳

Summer During the summer, performances of national
dances take place at the Museum of Seurasaari.
Information from the Curator, Kansallismuseo
(National Museum), Mannerheimintie 34, Helsinki (Helsingfors).

Winter Classes in national dancing can be seen through
the kindness of the Brage Bureau, Kaserngatan 28,
Helsingfors.

Also, Suomalaisen Kansantanssin Ystävät; inquire
at Helsinginkatu 11B, Helsinki.

Plate 2
South Karelia

THE DANCES

TECHNICAL EDITOR, MURIEL WEBSTER
ASSISTED BY KATHLEEN P. TUCK

ABBREVIATIONS
USED IN DESCRIPTION OF THE STEPS AND DANCES

r—right ⎱ referring to	R—right ⎱ describing turns or
l—left ⎰ hand, foot etc.	L—left ⎰ ground pattern
C—clockwise	C-C—counter-clockwise

For descriptions of foot positions and explanations of any ballet terms the following books are suggested for reference:

A Primer of Classical Ballet (Cecchetti method). Cyril Beaumont.

First Steps. Ruth French and Felix Demery.

The Ballet Lover's Pocket Book. Kay Ambrose.

REFERENCE BOOKS FOR DESCRIPTION OF FIGURES:

The Scottish Country Dance Society's Publications. Many volumes, from Thornhill, Cairnmuir Road, Edinburgh 12.

The English Folk Dance and Song Society's Publications. Cecil Sharp House, 2 Regent's Park Road, London N.W.1.

The Country Dance Book I–VI. Cecil J. Sharp. Novello & Co., London.

The poise of the body should be natural and easy, and unless otherwise indicated the arms hang freely by the sides.

Different grips. Single hand grasp, double hand grasp, cross hand grasp, and arms linked are in use but need no explanation.

Ring grasp. Standing in a ring, dancers join hands and hold them shoulder high.

Thumb grasp. Usually taken by 2 men who stand r or l shoulders towards each other. If right they take a thumb grasp with r hands, palms together. The grip is made round the base of each other's thumb.

Double ring grasp. Each man places r hand in front of waist of girl on his right to grasp the next man's l hand, and his l hand in front of waist of girl on his left to grasp the next man's r hand. Each woman has her arms above those of the men and grasps the next woman's hand so that a double ring is formed.

Reel grasp. When dancing clockwise partners face each other and grasp l hands across while r hands are placed on partner's r shoulder. When dancing counter-clockwise r hands are grasped and l hands are placed on partner's l shoulder.

Basket grasp (4 dancers). The 2 men, standing opposite each other, grasp their own l wrist with their r hand, and with their l hand grasp the r wrist of the other man so that the joined wrists make a little square. The two women, standing opposite each other, thread their arms under the men's near arms and over the men's other arms to grasp them from above.

BASIC STEPS

Walking, running, gallop steps, hop steps, Waltz steps in 3/4 or 2/4, Polka steps and Schottische steps are in use but need no explanation.

Mazurka steps. Like the Polka step but danced in 3/4 time.

Jig step, 2/4.	*Beats*
r behind l foot,	1
hop forward on right,	and
simultaneously l foot	
swings behind r,	2
hop forward on l.	and

Polska Reel step (pivot).

(*a*) 2/4. When turning to the R in couples or dancing C-C in a ring, step on to r foot with a bent knee, keeping weight well over r foot. Push off with ball of l foot at same time lifting r foot slightly to replace it in the direction in which the movement is being made, the weight is taken well on r foot.

         1
        and
        2

(*b*) 3/4. The step on r foot is made on count 1 and held for count 2, and the push from the ball of the l foot on count 3.

N.B.—When travelling C in a ring or turning to L in couples the weight is on l foot and the push from ball of r foot.

Polska Change step to 3/4.
   When turning on the spot to the L or if
moving clockwise in a ring, a change of step
is made with l foot then a jump on to r foot
which passes in front of l in order to move | 1 and 2
further in the direction in which the step is | 3
progressing.

   The change of step is made with r foot
when turning to R in 2's or if moving C-C
in a ring.

Polkamazurka step, as in Själaskuttan.   In 3/8
time.   Described as for r foot.
   (*a*) The r foot is moved forward. | 1
   (*b*) Close l foot behind r with weight on l foot. | 2
   (*c*) At same time r foot swings forward. | and
   (*d*) Then hop forward on l foot bending r | 3
knee so that the r foot is brought back towards
the l leg.
   Repeat with r foot.

Gliding hops, as in Själaskuttan, 3/8.
   These steps are danced with gliding hops on
r foot; the tip of the l foot slides close to the
r foot after each hop.   3 hops to each bar of
music.

Polka Heel step, as in Kökar Engelska, 4/4.
   Like a Polka step but 1st step is made on the
heel.   (Described as for r foot.)

   The r foot is kicked backward and then | and
swings quickly round to the front.   Place r | 1
foot forward on the heel, close l foot behind | and
r foot, step forward r foot.   Hop on r foot at | 2

23

same time kicking l foot back in preparation and for a step forward on the heel to repeat the 3 and 4 step with the l foot. 2 Polka Heel steps to each bar.

N.B.—When danced on the spot the leg swinging before the Heel step enables the dancers to turn a little to the opposite side so that in making a Polka Heel step with the r foot the heel is placed a little across to the left side and there is slight contra-body movement to the R.

TANELI

Poor old Taneli (Daniel) is sad, the girls do not like him because he has only one eye.

Region   Suomi (Finland), widespread. Plates 1, 2 and 4 (b).

Music   Play three times, as written. The first and last four bars are not used in the actual dance.

Character   The interest of this dance lies in the mime which is described in the title and in the dance description.

Formation   One man (Taneli) and four girls. All face forward to begin.

TANELI

Allegro

Widespread in Suomi (Finland)

Dance.   *Play 3 times*   **A**

B

To end

	MUSIC
	Bars
FIGURE I	
1 8 stride jumps, turning to the L on the 2nd, 4th, 6th, 8th jump, so that a complete turn is made. Feet are jumped about 18 inches apart, then together, once to each bar.	1–8
2 Repeat turning to R.	9–16
FIGURE II	
1 Taneli becomes distressed because he can never see the girls' faces, so he dances twice as quickly, i.e. 2 complete stride jumps to each bar. The girls copy him, turning on every second jump, thus still turning away from him.	1–16
FIGURE III	
1 Same as figure 1. Taneli gets very dejected and knees begin to sag. At the end he walks away, falls on his knees or on to the floor and surrenders to his grief, but the girls repent and help him to his feet.	1–16

SAHAN KATRILLI. *Saw Quadrille*

Region Suomi (Finland), widespread. Plates 1, 2 and 4(b).

Character Walking steps. Rather stately.

Formation For 4 or more couples standing facing each other in two parallel lines, each woman on R of partner.

```
     4        1
     □   ○   □   ○
                      FRONT
     ○   □   ○   □
     3        2
```

	MUSIC
	Bars
FIGURE I	**A**
1 With hands joined along each line on a level with the shoulders all move away from the front with 6 walking steps.	1–2
2 All move 3 steps towards the front.	3
3 Repeat movements of bars 1–3.	4–6
4 All move 3 steps away from front.	7
5 All lean away from the front with toe of foot nearest front on the ground.	8

N.B.—Throughout this figure the end dancers have their hands on their hips, and dancers start on foot farthest away from the front.

SAHAN KATRILLI

A *1st figure* Stately

B *2nd figure*

C *3rd figure*

28

		B
FIGURE II		
1	Lines move towards each other with 4 steps.	9–10
2	Move 4 steps away from each other.	11–12
3	Couples standing opposite each other change places with 8 steps, each couple keeping to the L.	13–16
4	Repeat the movements of bars 9–16, couples crossing back into places.	9–16

		C
FIGURE III		
1	1st and 4th men and 2nd and 3rd women join hands in a ring and move round to the L, to pause for a moment in the diagonally opposite place, so that all the girls are in one	17–20

Plate 3
Aland (man)

East Bothnia: Munsala (woman)

a

b

a

b

Plate 4
Satakunta

line and all the men in the other. All make
a slight bow to opposite partners.

2 Joining in a ring again and moving in the
same direction, dance to own places. | 21–24

3 2nd and 3rd men and 1st and 4th women
repeat same movement. | 17–24

FIGURE IV | D

1 Each man joins both hands with the girl | 25–28
opposite and they dance round together on
the spot C-C for 8 steps.

2 Repeat moving C. | 29–32

3 Repeat movements of bars 25–32 with own | 25–32
partner.

The dance is then repeated from the
beginning.

Note.—This Sahan Katrilli, or Saw Quadrille, is a good
example of the composite dances of Finland. It
is of more interest than some of the numberless
descendants of the once-fashionable Quadrille on
account of its variety of time signatures. Note its
opening in 3/4, a transitional bar in 4/4 taking the
rhythm into a simple 2/4 beat for the second figure.
Its regulation four figures are still reminiscent of
the ballroom Quadrille.

KÖKAR ENGELSKA. *English dance from Kökar*

Region — Kökar, Åland. Swedish-speaking parts of Finland. Plates 3 and 4(a).

Character — Lively.

Formation — For an even number of couples standing in 2 lines, facing each other and about 4 steps away. Girls stand in L line and men in R line when looked at from the front.

```
O→   ← O      O→   ← O
                              FRONT
□→   ← □      □→   ← □
4      3        2      1
```

	MUSIC Bars
FIGURE I Ring	A
1 With hands joined and lifted to shoulder level, all move C in a ring with 8 Polka Heel steps, starting with the l foot.	1–4
2 Still keeping hands joined, repeat movements of bars 1–4 moving C-C and end in 2 lines again.	1–4
FIGURE II Figure	B
1 All dance 6 Polka Heel steps in place starting with l foot, girls with arms hanging naturally by their sides, the men beckoning alternately with r or l hands as if calling the girls who are refusing.	5–7

2 Change places with partners with 2 Polka Heel steps. Men have thumbs in armholes, girls arms akimbo. Each dancer keeps to the right so that partners pass l shoulders and on the second step each dancer turns to the L to end in partner's place. | 8

3 Repeat movements of bars 5–8 back to own place closing in lines and facing in 2's along each line. | 5–8

FIGURE III   Winding—Polka Heel step
During this figure the girls dance with arms akimbo and men with thumbs in armholes. Straight hey on each side, dancers starting l foot and passing r shoulders with the dancers they are facing. If 8 couples dance they should all be back in their own place by the end of the 16th Polka Heel step. If there are more or fewer couples they will remain in the place they reach on the 16th step. | A 1–4 1–4

FIGURE IV. Repeat movements of Fig. II (5–8) (5–8). | B

FIGURE V. Repeat movements of Fig. III (1–4) (1–4). | A

FIGURE VI. Repeat movements of Fig. II (5–8) (5–8). | B

FIGURE VII. Repeat movements of Fig. I (1–4) (1–4). | A

The dance ends with all the dancers holding hands in a ring with the hands at shoulder height.

34

The music sequence runs A A B B, A A B B, A A B B, A A.

35

SJÄLASKUTTAN. *The Seals' Jump*

Region	Kimito, Åboland. Swedish-speaking parts of Finland. Plates 3 and 4(a).
Character	Somewhat heavy, imitating seals.
Formation	For any number of couples standing one behind the other with inside hand grasp and outside hand on the hip.

```
O       O       O       O       O
<       <       <       <       <
□       □       □       □       □
```

	MUSIC *Bars*
FIGURE I	
1 Starting with outside foot 3 Polkamazurka steps forward.	1–3
2 Step on to outside foot and then bring the feet together with a jump, bending the knees and pausing to face each other.	4
3 Repeat the movements of bars 1–4 but on jump turn away from each other.	5–8
4 1 Polkamazurka step with outside foot.	9
5 Step on to outside foot and jump to face each other again with feet together and knees bent.	10
6 Repeat movements of bars 9 and 10 but on jump turn away from each other.	11–12

36

SJÄLASKUTTAN

From Kimito, Åboland

Well marked. M.M. ♩ = 152.

Play twice through

37

7 Starting with outside foot 3 Polkamazurka steps.   13–15

8 Step on to outside foot and then jump with feet together facing partner again.   16

9 Repeat movements of bars 1–16, 1st couple leading down the centre away from the front to end in 2 lines about 4 steps apart—girls in L line and men in R line when looked at from the front.   1–16

FIGURE II

Throughout this figure all lift the arms so that the elbows are on a level with the shoulders, with the hands hanging slackly down from the wrists in front of the chest to represent the fins of a seal.

1 The 2 lines dance towards each other with 3 gliding steps on r foot.   1

2 Join both hands with partner, elbows still on shoulder level, and dance once round on the spot with 3 gliding steps on r foot.   2

3 Move back to place with 3 gliding steps.   3

4 Jump with the feet together as long as it pleases the musician to repeat the last note of the bar.   4

5 Repeat the movements of bars 1–4.   5–8

6 Lines move towards each other with 4 gliding steps, then jump with feet together, turning about, men to L and girls to R, to finish back to back.   9–10

7 Stand back to back.   11

8 Jump again with feet together, men to R and   12
girls to L, to finish facing partner.

     N.B.—The jump is made on the last note
of bars 10 and 12.

9 Join both hands and swing once round   13–14
C on spot with 6 gliding steps.

10 Let go hands and dance backward with 3   15
gliding steps as in bar 2.

11 Jump on spot with feet together as long as   16
it pleases the musician to repeat the last
note of bar 16.

    Repeat the whole dance.

❧ NOTE ❧

*We beg our readers not to think of regional costumes as fancy
dress. They are held in honour by their wearers as an important
part of their heritage. Respect them. Do not dress dancers in a
make-believe Scandinavian costume for these Finnish dances. You
would be equally justified in dressing a Helston Furry dancer in a
Highland kilt.*

The Editor

BIBLIOGRAPHY

BURCHENAL, ELIZABETH.—*Folk-dances of Finland.* G. Schirmer, New York, 1915. (Tunes and descriptions of 66 dances.)

COLLAN, ANNI.—*Suomalainen Kisapirtti* (new edition). V. Söderström, Helsinki, 1946. (Tunes and descriptions of 67 dances.)

HEIKEL, YNGVAR (ed.).—*Folkdansbeskrivningar.* Publications of Svenska Litteratursällskapet i Finland, Vol. 268. Helsingfors, 1938. (Descriptions of 123 dances, and some tunes.)

KROHN, ILMARI (ed.).—*Kansantansseja.* Suomalaisen Kirjallisuuden Seuda (Society of Finnish Literature), Helsinki, 1893. (668 folk-dance tunes.)

PULKKINEN, ASKO.—*Suomalaisia Kansantanhuja* (new edition). V. Söderström, Helsinki, 1946. (Tunes and descriptions of 56 dances.)

RANTA, SULHO.—*Suomalaisia Kansantanhusävelmiä.* V. Söderström, Helsinki, 1936. (Folk-dance arranged for piano and two violins.)

SIRELIUS, U. T.—*Suomen Kansallispukuja,* I and II. Otava, Helsinki, 1921. (Drawings of 16 folk costumes.)

VAHTER, TYYNI, and STRANDBERG, GRETA.—*Suomen Kansallispukuja.* V. Söderström, Helsinki, 1936. (15 national costumes of Suomi.)

VÄISÄNEN, A. O. (ed.).—*Kantele- ja jouhikkosävelmiä.* Suomalaisen Kirjallisuuden Seura, Helsinki, 1928. (Folk-dance tunes for *kantele* and violin.)